Butterfly Mandala Adult (… 2

60 Beautiful Butterfly Desi … icate Patterns For Stress Relief

By Omar Johnson

Get Your Free Mandala

Visit

ADULTCOLORINGBOOKSFORYOU.COM

Make Profits Easy LLC Publishing

profitsdaily123@aol.com

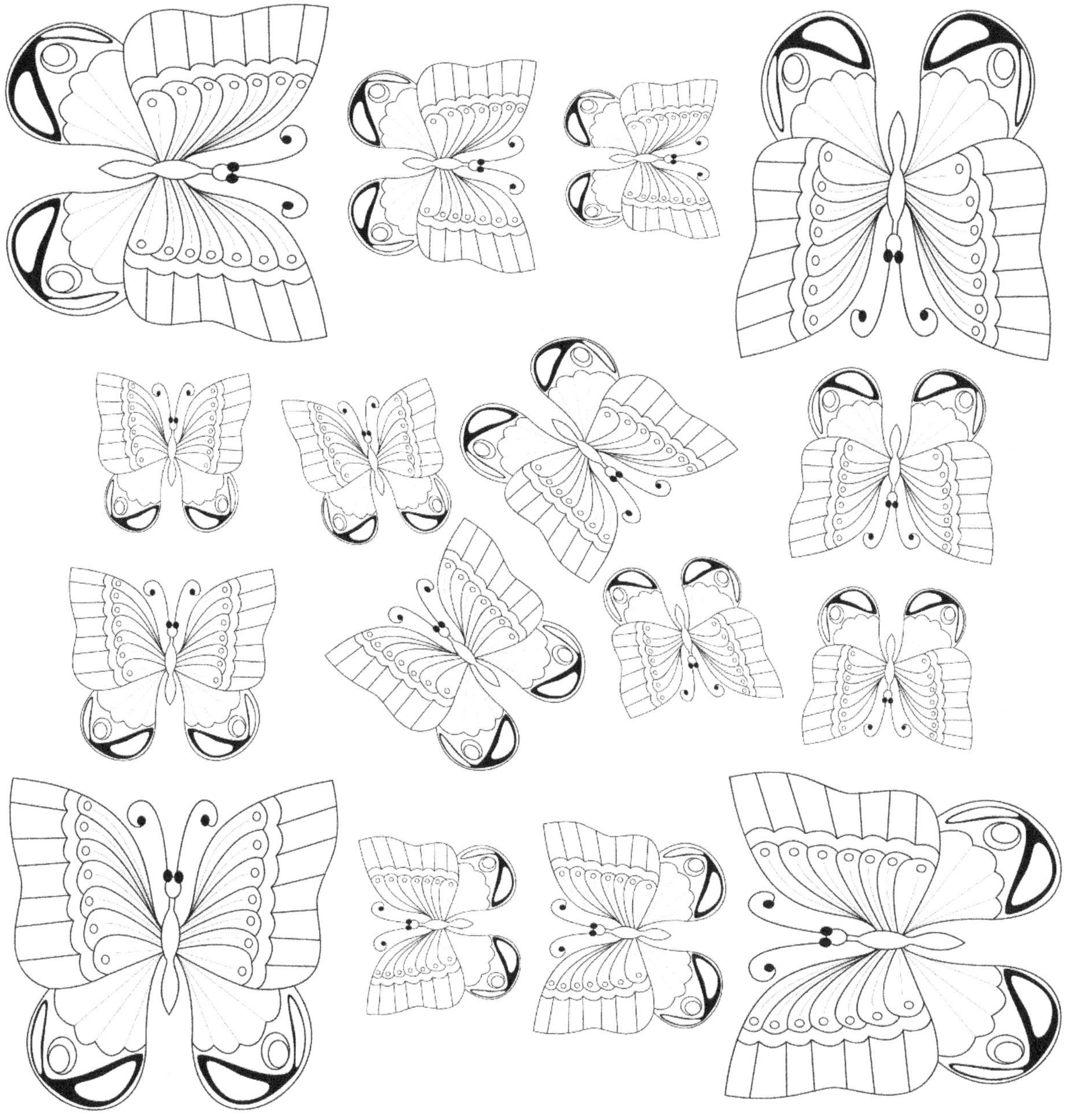

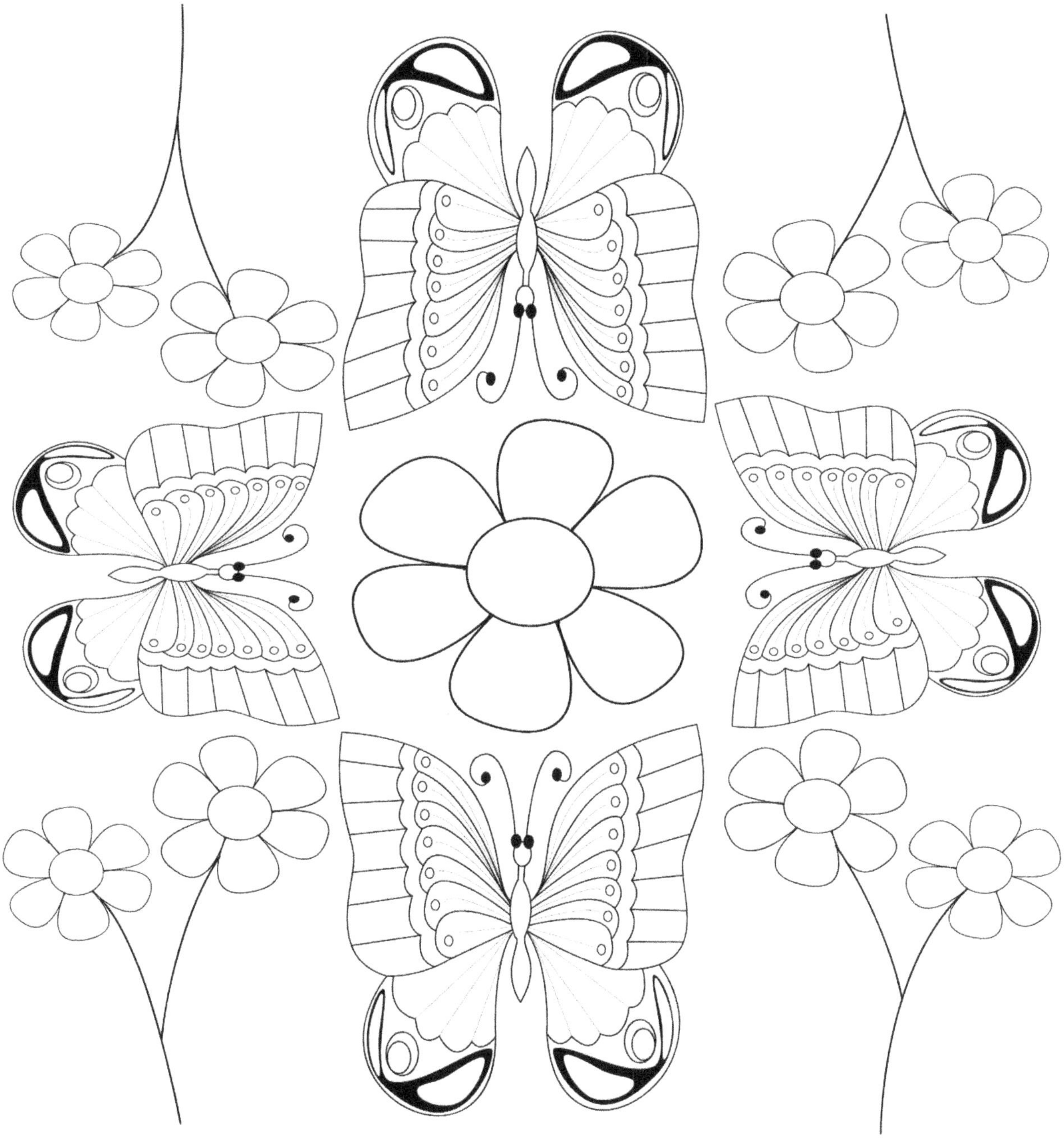

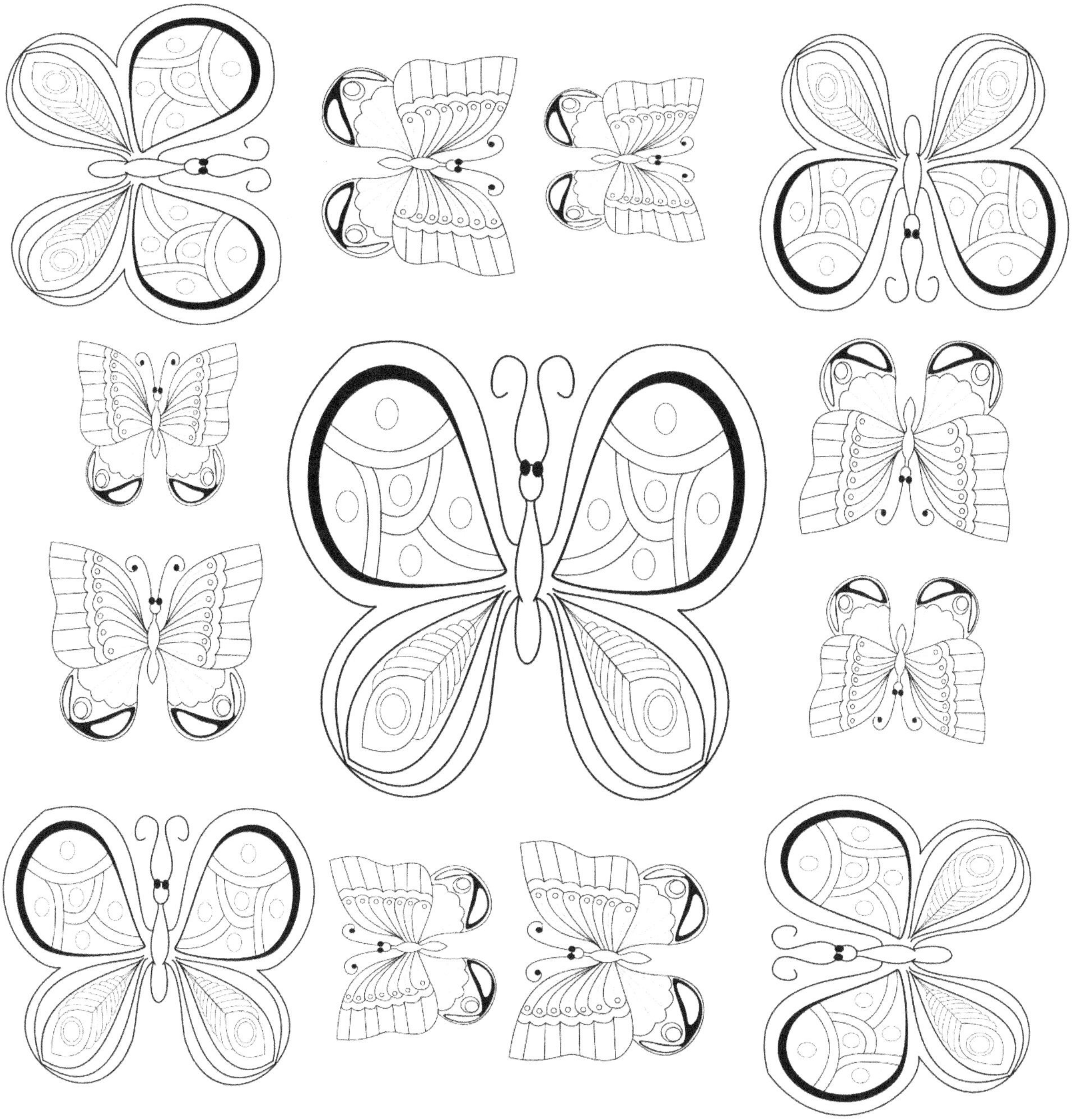

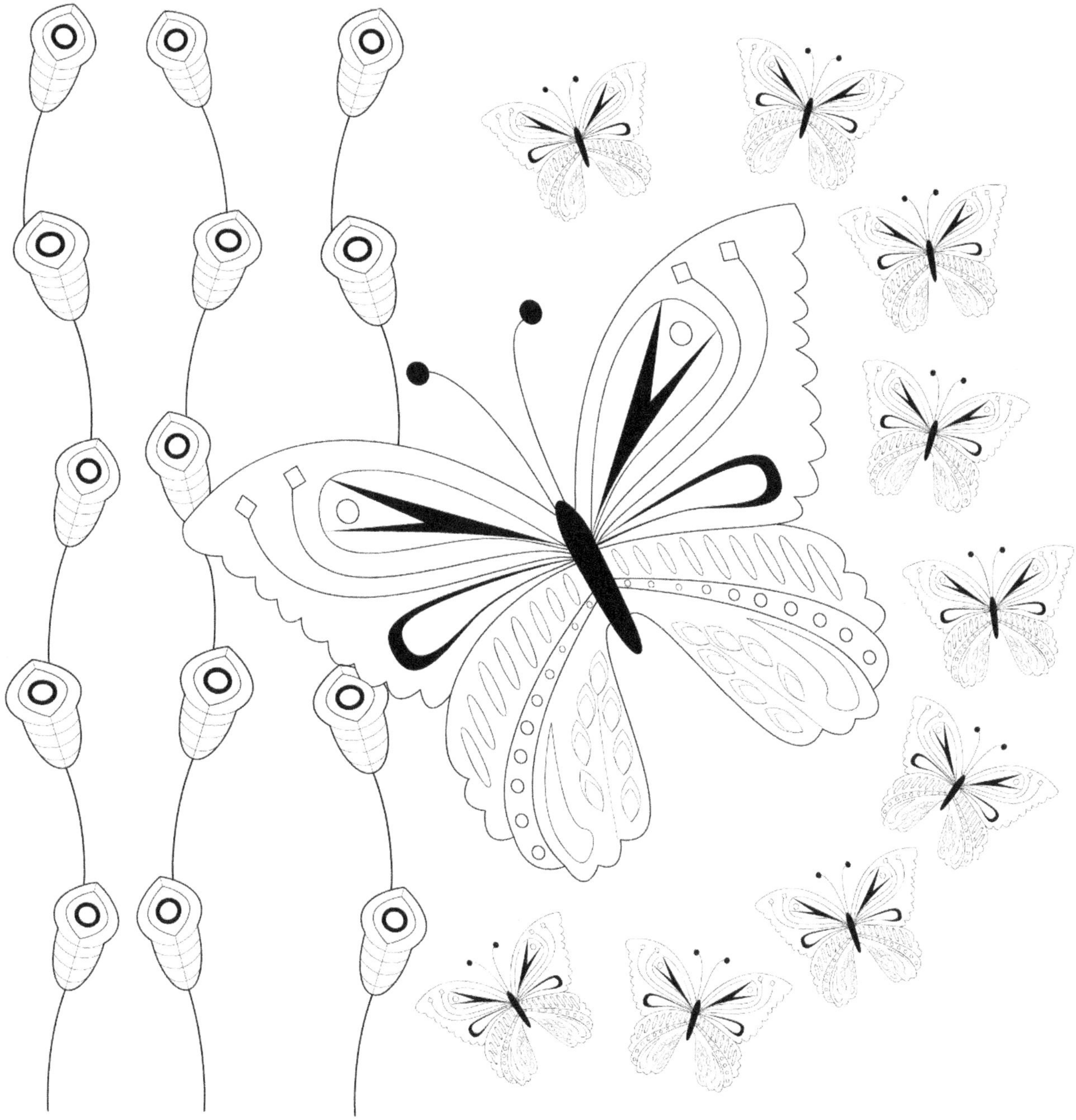

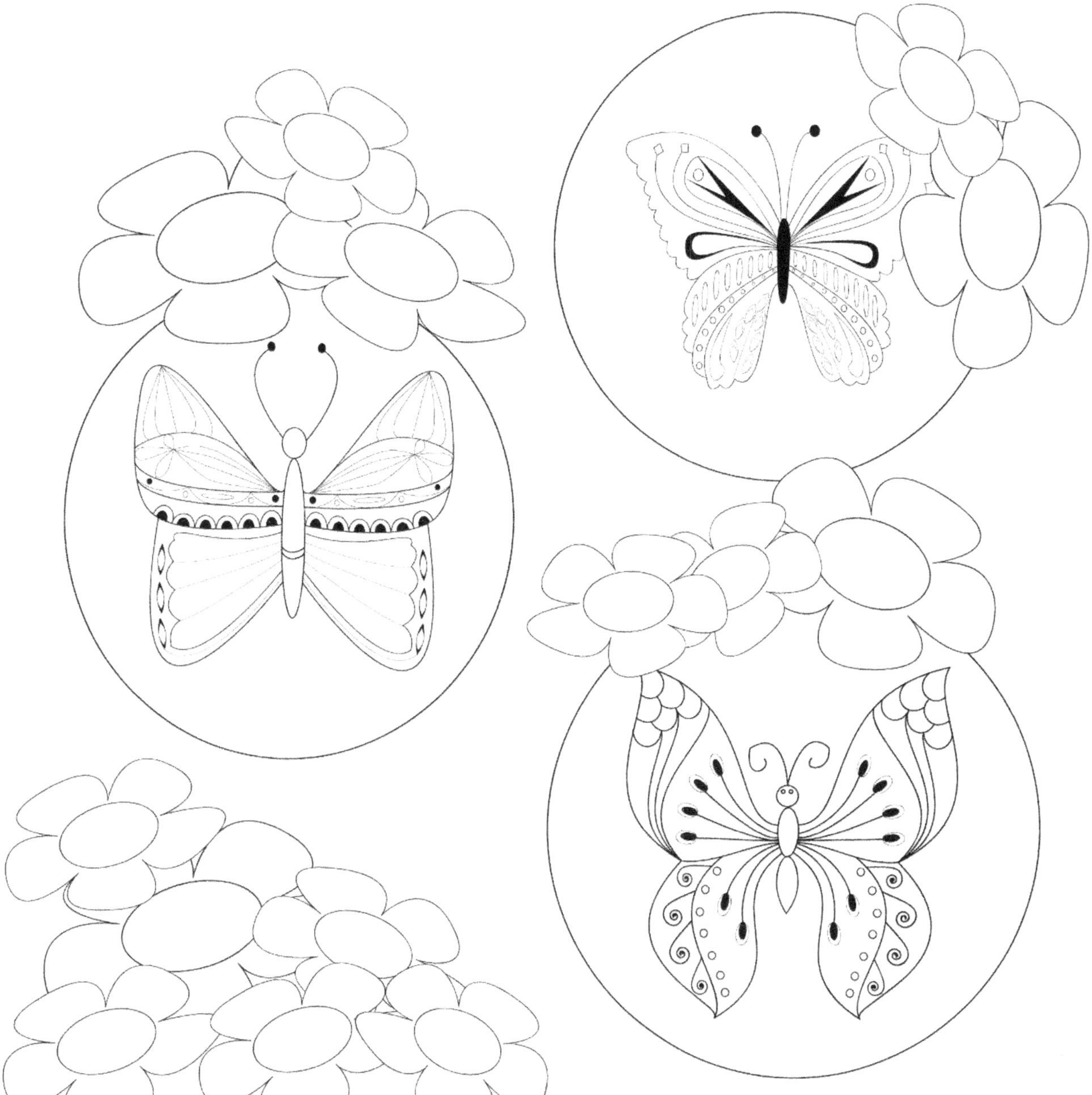

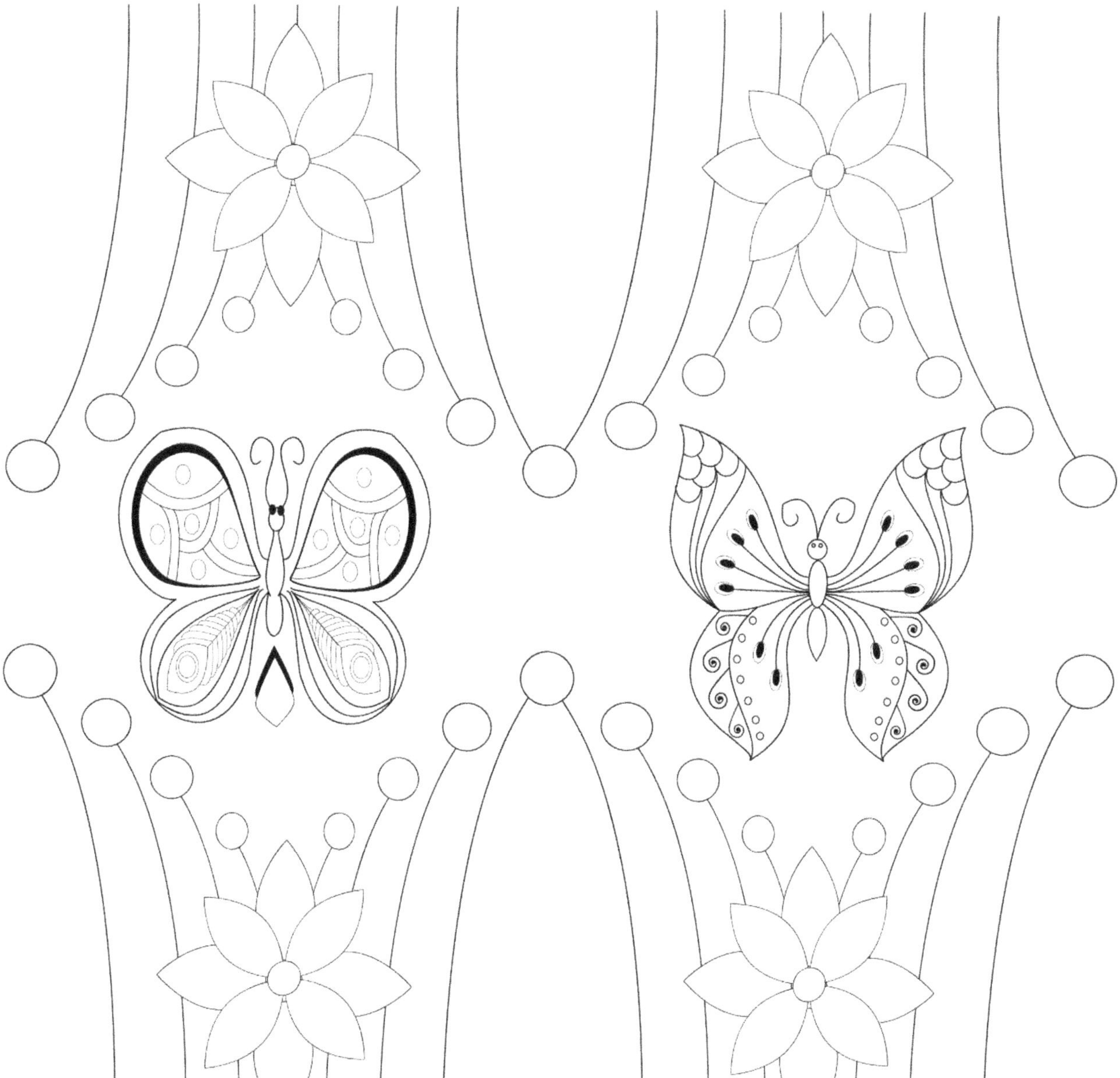

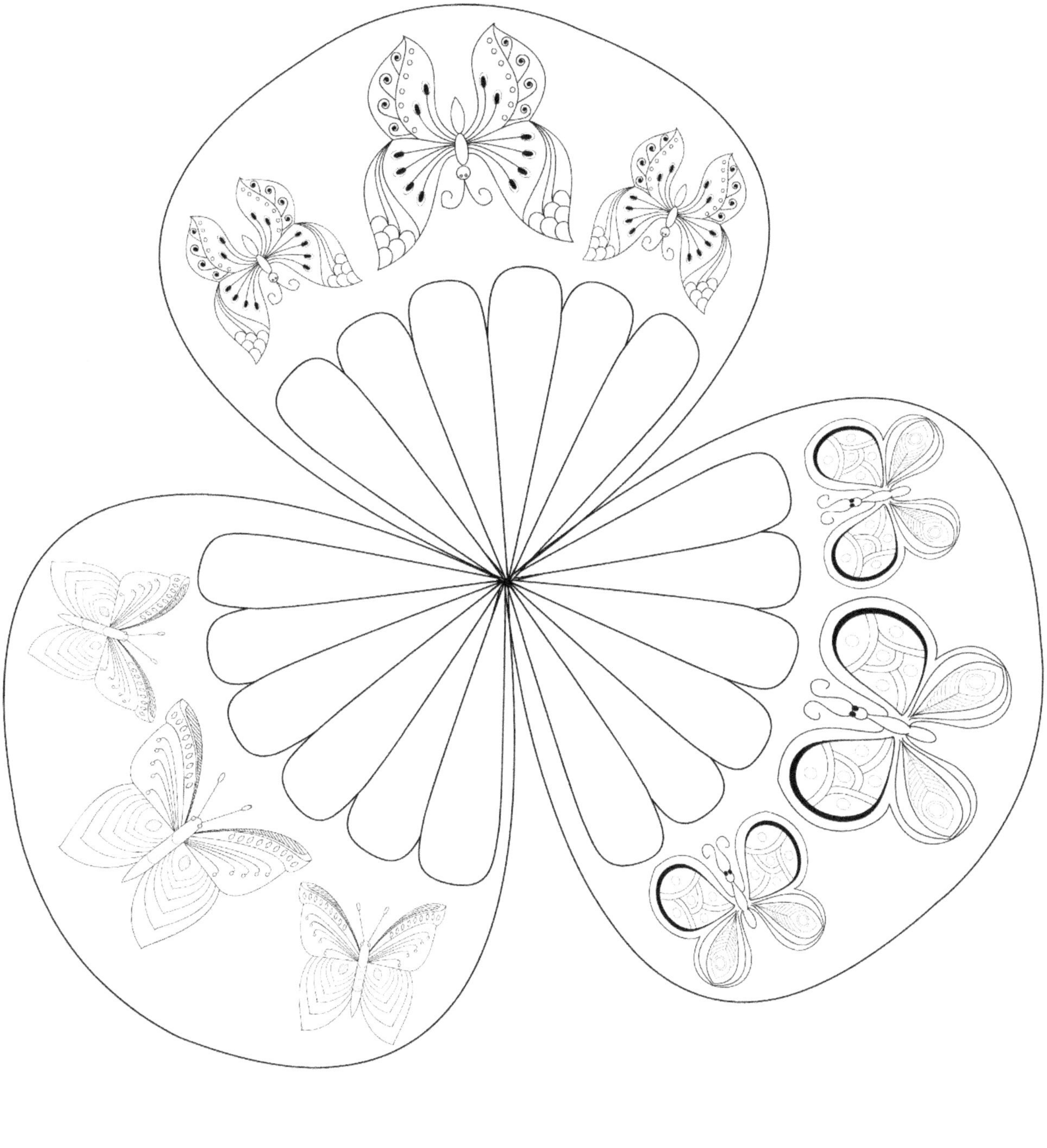